OMIMIDS

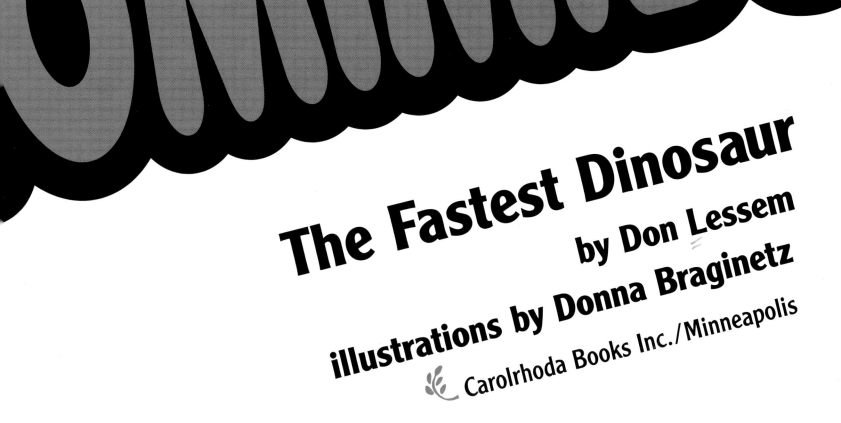

The Fastest Dinosaur

by Don Lessem

illustrations by Donna Braginetz

Carolrhoda Books Inc./Minneapolis

Special thanks to Dr. Philip J. Currie, Head of
Dinosaur Research, Royal Tyrrell Museum of
Paleontology, for his invaluable help in the
preparation of this book.

Carolrhoda Books, Inc. c/o The Lerner Group
241 First Avenue North, Minneapolis, MN 55401

Library of Congress Cataloging-in-Publication Data

Lessem, Don.
    Ornithomimids, the fastest dinosaur / by Don Lessem ; illustrations
by Donna Braginetz
        p.   cm.—(Special Dinosaurs)
    Includes index.
    Summary: Describes the research and paleontological investigation
that led to the identification and classification of ornithomimid
dinosaurs.
    ISBN 0-87614-813-5
    1. Ornithomimidae—Juvenile literature. [1. Ornithomimus.
2. Dinosaurs. 3. Paleontology. 4. Fossils.] I. Braginetz, Donna, ill.
II. Title. III. Series.
QE862.S3L46 1995
567.9'7—dc20   93-10264
                                                              CIP
                                                              AC

Manufactured in the United States of America
1 2 3 4 5 6 - JR - 01 00 99 98 97 96

To Bill Gross, a friend of dinosaurs, education, and children, big and small—D. L.

To Mom and Dad—D. B.

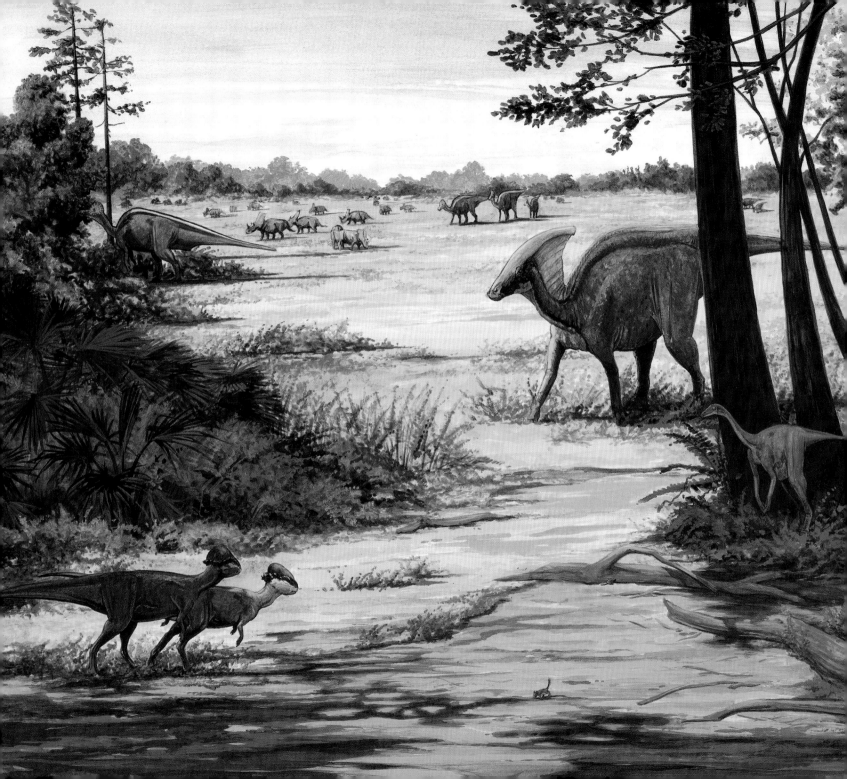

It is late afternoon in western Canada, 67 million years ago. The sun is setting over a huge plain near the ocean shore. Browsing on the plain are vast herds of duckbilled and horned dinosaurs. They munch noisily on trees, bushes, and ground plants. Smaller **herbivorous** (er-BIH-vuh-ruhs), or plant-eating, dinosaurs, some with thick dome heads, also nibble at plants. Furry mammals the size of rats dart in and out of the bushes. In-sects flit through the air. As they feed, all these animals are alert to what's going on around them. The plant-eaters know that there may be **predators** nearby look-ing for them. Among the dangerous hunters roaming the land is *Tyranno-saurus rex.* Forty-five feet long, with teeth the size of bananas, this dinosaur is per-haps the biggest meat-eater that ever walked the Earth.

A reconstructed *Tyrannosaurus rex* skeleton

But the little mammals and the insects are on the lookout for another hunter. This dinosaur is not very big—only 11 feet long—but it is fast. It has little to fear from *Tyrannosaurus rex* or any other dinosaur because it can outrun any animal in its world.

One of these swift predators is hunting now, looking out from behind a tree. With its large eyes, the dinosaur spots a mammal feeding in the open. Sprinting on long legs, it races toward the little mammal. The frightened animal darts for its hole, but it is no match for a dinosaur that runs as fast as a race horse.

In an instant, the dinosaur has caught up to its prey and grabbed it with the three clawed fingers of one of its gripping hands. The hungry racer stuffs the little animal into its mouth.

What is this speedy killer? It is *Ornith-omimus* (OR-nith-oh-MY-mus), a name that means "bird mimic." The dinosaur looks very much like one particular bird, the ostrich. Like an ostrich, *Ornithomimus* has a long neck, long legs, and a toothless beak.

What *Ornithomimus* doesn't look much like is our popular image of a dinosaur. It is difficult for many people to imagine a hunting dinosaur without teeth. We usually think of hunters as having dagger-sharp teeth. And most of us don't think of dinosaurs running on two legs at speeds faster than a human's.

As you can see from this drawing, ornithomimid dinosaurs were built somewhat like ostriches, with long legs, long necks, and toothless beaks.

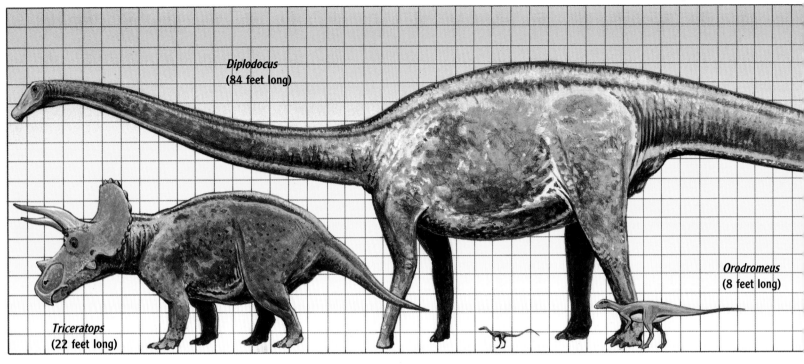

Diplodocus
(84 feet long)

Triceratops
(22 feet long)

Orodromeus
(8 feet long)

Compsognathus
(3⅓ feet long)

Dinosaurs came in a variety of sizes, from smaller than an average human to many times bigger. Each square in the grid represents 1 foot.

When dinosaurs were first discovered in the 1820s, people thought they were sluggish animals that lumbered along on all fours. They seemed to have a lot in common with lizards. In fact, the name dinosaur means "terrible lizard." Like lizards, dinosaurs were thought to be cold-blooded animals and thus less active than warm-blooded animals such as birds and mammals.

We've learned a lot since the 1840s, and we now know that dinosaurs are much more complicated than people first thought. Scientists have discovered more than 300 different kinds of dinosaurs from over 150 million years of Earth history. Some were huge. Others were as small as chickens. Some dinosaurs were

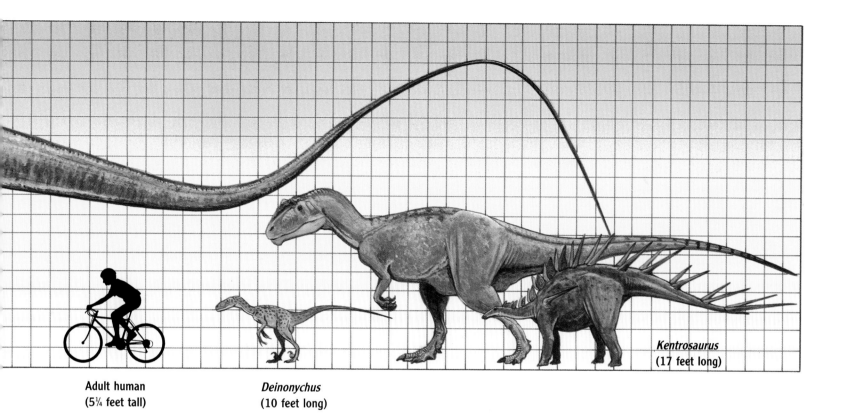

Adult human
(5¼ feet tall)

Deinonychus
(10 feet long)

Kentrosaurus
(17 feet long)

probably slow-moving and not very smart. But others were faster and smarter than any other animals of their time.

We also know that, despite their name, dinosaurs weren't lizards. They developed more than 225 million years ago from the same animals that were the ancestors of lizards and other reptiles. But dinosaurs belong to their own group. Many features made them different from reptiles. For example, dinosaurs walked with their legs held straight underneath their bodies. Lizards have bowed legs, and they waddle when they walk. The straight-legged position helped some dinosaurs to be speedy runners.

The closest living relatives of dinosaurs like *Ornithomimus* and other meat-eaters are not modern lizards, snakes, and crocodiles. They are birds. Like birds, these dinosaurs had hollow bones. And like birds, they were probably warm-blooded. Their body temperatures stayed the same instead of rising and falling with the temperature of their surroundings. A dinosaur's temperature-regulating system may have been different from those of birds and mammals. But like some of these warm-blooded animals, some dinosaurs could have had the energy to run long distances at high speeds.

A herd of ostriches in Kenya. Ostriches and other birds are the closest living relatives of meat-eating dinosaurs, including ornithomimids.

Dr. Othniel Charles Marsh (top) and his rival, Dr. Edward Drinker Cope

Dinosaurs made up a very special group of animals. And among the most unusual of all dinosaurs were *Ornithomimus* and its close relatives, the ornithomimids. Although we have known about the ornithomimids for a long time, they remain puzzling animals.

The first ornithomimid was named in 1890 by a man who discovered and named more dinosaurs than anyone else in history. He was Othniel Charles Marsh, a professor at Yale University in Connecticut. Dr. Marsh was a bitter rival of another scientist, Edward Drinker Cope, who lived in Philadelphia. During the late 1800s, these two men started a **fossil**-collecting race to find and name as many dinosaurs as possible.

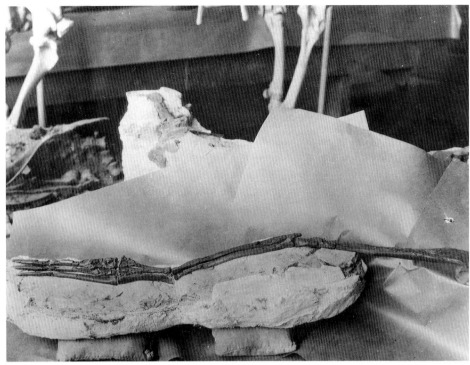

A front leg, or forelimb, of an *Ornithomimus*

Opposite page: Duckbilled dinosaurs such as *Edmontosaurus* (top left) and *Maisaura* (top right) had three-toed feet. Many theropods, including *Tyrannosaurus rex,* had three large toes that touched the ground plus one small, raised toe.

In 1889, one of Professor Marsh's collectors, George Cannon, was working in Colorado at the foothills of the Rocky Mountains. Here he found pieces of an unknown dinosaur's foot. The fossil foot was narrow and graceful and had three toes. It looked like the foot of a fast-running bird, so Professor Marsh called the dinosaur *Ornithomimus velox,* "speedy bird mimic."

For a long time, no one was sure where *Ornithomimus* fit into the dinosaur family tree. Professor Marsh first thought that it could be a relative of the duckbilled dinosaurs, a group that includes big plant-eaters like *Maiasaura* and *Edmontosaurus.* Duckbills have three-toed feet. Later Marsh decided that *Ornithomimus* might be a **theropod,** or "beast-foot" dinosaur. *Tyrannosaurus rex* and all the other **carnivores** (KAR-nuh-vorz), or meat-eaters, are theropods. Many members of the group have narrow feet with three large toes, just like *Ornithomimus.*

Henry Fairfield Osborn

When Professor Osborn examined *Struthiomimus*, he found that the animal was more than 11 feet long. It was shaped much like the running birds of today, with a small head and long neck and legs. Like modern birds, it had no teeth. Professor Osborn decided that both *Struthiomimus* and *Ornithomimus* belonged to a special group of bird-like dinosaurs, which he called ornithomimids.

Since the time of Dr. Osborn, we have learned a lot about ornithomimids—what they were like and when and where they lived. It turns out that the first ornithomimid found was one of the last of the group. In fact, it was one of the last dinosaurs on Earth, as far as we know. *Ornithomimus velox* lived in the American West about 65 million years ago, around the time that dinosaurs became extinct.

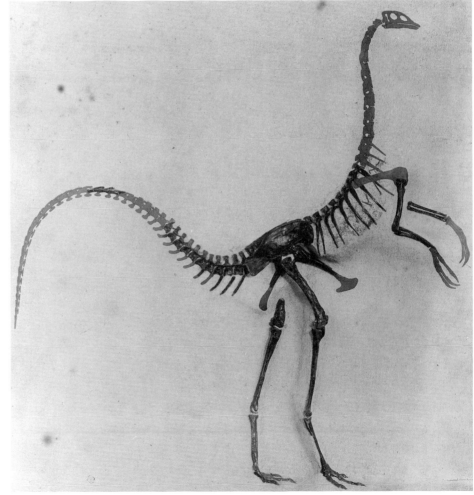

A *Struthiomimus* skeleton

The earliest ornithomimid we know is *Harpymimus*, found in 1984. It is about 115 million years old and comes not from North America but from the Gobi Desert of Mongolia in Central Asia. Mongolian scientists named *Harpymimus* after a mythical monster called a harpy. This dinosaur is no monster, but it is strange. *Harpymimus* is a small ornithomimid with short arms and thick feet. And it has teeth! There are six small, blunt teeth at the front of its jaw.

Harpymimus has an important place in the evolution of the ornithomimids. It developed from the toothy meat-eating dinosaurs that were the ancestors of all ornithomimids. After *Harpymimus*, ornithomimids became toothless animals like *Struthiomimus*.

Members of the ornithomimid family. *Left to right: Ornithomimus; Gallimimus; Harpymimus; Struthiomimus; Timimus; Dromiceiomimus*

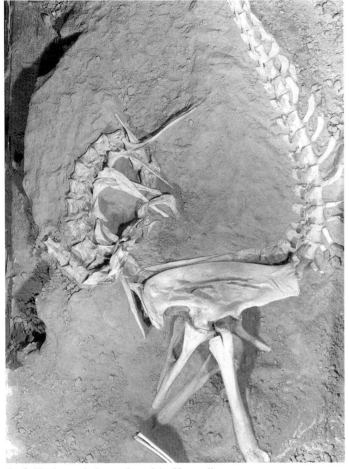

A *Gallimimus* skeleton found in Mongolia

The Gobi Desert of Mongolia is one of the best places in the world for finding ornithomimids. The most spectacular discoveries made there include several nearly complete skeletons of a huge ornithomimid. They belong to *Gallimimus*, the biggest of all the bird-mimic dinosaurs. *Gallimimus* was nearly 20 feet long! It was named by a woman scientist from Poland, Halszka Osmolska, who explored the Gobi Desert in the late 1960s and early 1970s.

More ornithomimids have also been found in North America since the first ones were discovered a century ago. In 1933, the skulls and parts of the skeletons of a second species of *Ornithomimus* were found in Alberta, Canada. From the same area have come skulls and skeletal parts of another kind of ornithomimid. Its name is *Dromiceiomimus*, and it was a very light, long-legged dinosaur. More than 11 feet long, it probably weighed no more than 220 pounds. *Dromiceiomimus* may have been the fastest of all the ornithomimids.

Fossils found in Europe suggest that ornithomimids may have lived there too. And a new ornithomimid-like dinosaur has been found in Australia. It has been named *Timimus hermani*, in honor of Tim, the young son of Pat Vickers-Rich and Tom Rich, the scientists who discovered it.

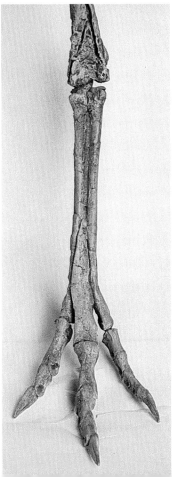

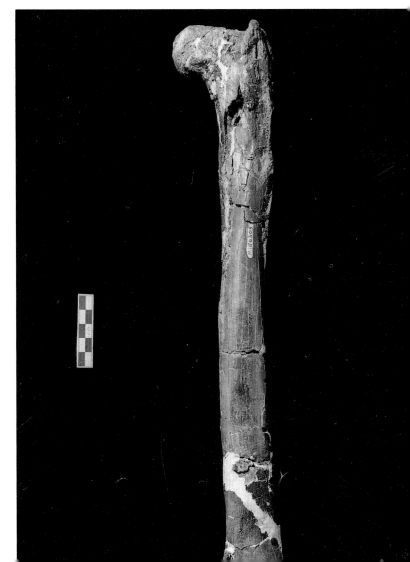

Left: A *Dromiceiomimus* skull (top) and leg (bottom). *Below:* A legbone of *Timimus hermani,* the most recently identified ornithomimid.

These maps show how the Earth might have looked about 200 million years ago (top), when the continents formed a single mass that scientists call Pangaea, and during the Cretaceous period (bottom), about 80 million years ago.

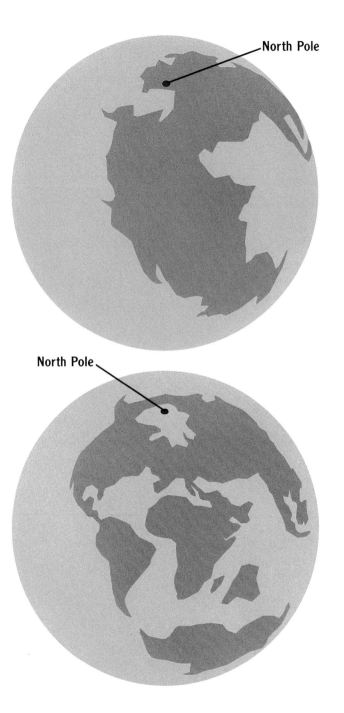

North Pole

North Pole

Ornithomimids have been found in North America, Europe, Asia, and Australia. How could they have lived in so many different places around the world? Until about 190 million years ago, all of Earth's continents were joined in one huge land mass, called **Pangaea** (pan-JEE-uh). During this period, it was possible for the same dinosaurs to spread all over the planet. Later, during the **Cretaceous** (krih-TAY-shus) period (144 to 65 million years ago), the land mass split up into the continents we know now. During this time, different kinds of dinosaurs developed on each continent.

So why have scientists found ornithomimids from the Cretaceous period in both Asia and North America? During this period, the two continents were connected by land in the arctic region. Dinosaurs could move back and forth between them. This explains why Mongolia had dinosaurs that looked very much like American dinosaurs from the Cretaceous period such as the duckbills, *Tyrannosaurus rex*, and *Ornithomimus*.

The Cretaceous ornithomimids in Asia and North America lived in very different environments. Around 65 million years ago, the ornithomimids of western Canada lived on a coastal plain. Plant life was rich, and the climate was as warm and humid as it is in Florida today. At the same time in Mongolia, the weather was drier, with alternating dry and wet seasons.

Some Cretaceous dinosaurs don't seem to have liked the Mongolian climate. Horned dinosaurs like *Triceratops,* which were so common in North America, have rarely been found in Asia. But these climate differences apparently didn't bother the ornithomimids. One reason they could

Ornithomimids probably had strong, flexible beaks covering their jaws, much like the parrot pictured above.

survive in such different environments may have been because they ate many kinds of food.

We know that most ornithomimids had no teeth to cut and grind food. So how did they eat? Scientists believe that, because of the thinness and lightness of their skulls, the dinosaurs probably had very flexible jaws. Those jaws were covered with horny beaks, like those of birds. With its beak, an ornithomimid could have cut up food without the help of teeth. Like some birds, it might have been able to move food around in its mouth with great precision. A parrot can use its beak to open a sunflower seed and spit out the shell.

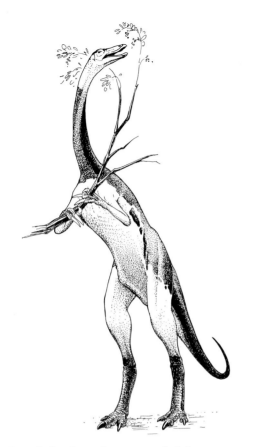

they collected by wading in shallow water. Today many long-legged birds—for example, flamingoes and herons—feed in this way. For ornithomimids, water animals would have been more like the diet of their meat-eating ancestors than plants would have been.

Scientists have had several different theories about how and what ornithomimids ate. Some thought they ate plants and leaves from trees; others believed they ate crabs and shrimps in shallow water, like some present-day birds do. A third theory was that they took in insects with their tongues, as anteaters (opposite page) do.

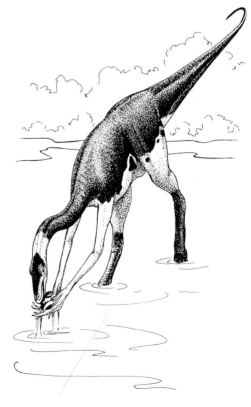

Flexible beaks would have permitted ornithomimids to eat many foods. But which foods would the dinosaurs have chosen? Professor Osborn (the scientist who discovered *Struthiomimus*) thought that they ate plants. He pictured ornithomimids pulling down branches with their arms and biting them off with their beaks.

Other scientists of his time had different ideas. Osborn's chief fossil collector, Barnum Brown, thought that ornithomimids ate crabs and shrimps, which

Another scientist of the early 1900s suggested that since ornithomimids had no teeth, they might have gotten their food as modern anteaters do. These toothless animals dig out insects and lick them up with sticky tongues.

But there's no evidence that ornithomimids had the powerful shoulder muscles needed for digging. Muscles leave marks on bones that tell us their shape and size. Ornithomimid bones don't show the marks of big muscles. It's hard to say what kind of tongues ornithomimids had. Soft body parts like tongues don't often become fossils.

Opposite page: Most scientists now believe that ornithomimids were omnivores, eating a variety of foods.

Dr. William King Gregory, a scientist of Osborn's time, thought that ornithomimids had a varied diet. He suggested that they were **omnivores** (AHM-nih-vorz), eating fruits, seeds, insects, and small animals. Today we still don't know exactly what ornithomimids ate, but most scientists accept Dr. Gregory's theory. They believe that these dinosaurs ate many kinds of food, including mouse-sized mammals and flying insects.

Ornithomimids could have caught and eaten these fast-moving creatures because the dinosaurs were fast themselves. Their bones tell us that. Like ostriches, which race at speeds over 30 miles an hour, ornithomimids were built to run fast.

Almost every part of the skeleton of *Ornithomimus* seems to have been designed with rapid movement in mind. The animal's long tail was very stiff and straight. With its tail held out straight like the rudder on a ship, *Ornithomimus* could stay balanced while running fast. (Ostriches have stubby tails, but they flap their wings for balance.)

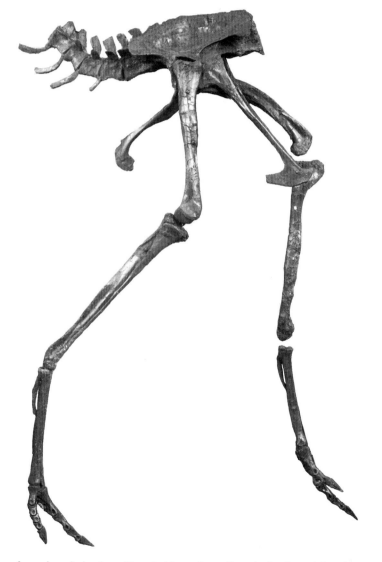

Long legs helped ornithomimids such as *Dromiceiomimus* (above).

27

An *Ornithomimus* running

Ornithomimus's running power came from its long, slender hind legs. These legs were built lightly for running. They weren't made to support a lot of weight, like the legs of *Brachiosaurus* and other heavy dinosaurs.

Let's take a look at one of *Ornithomimus's* legs, starting at the foot and working our way up to the hip. At the tip of the toes, we can see narrow claws that are flat on the bottom. When the dinosaur ran, these claws could have gripped the ground to stop the foot from sliding backwards.

The three toes on an ornithomimid's foot were unusually long and slender. So were the upper foot bones and lower leg bones. These are all features of fast-moving animals. Cheetahs, the fastest animal runners today, have the longest lower legs for their size of any cat. Even among people, those with longer lower legs are usually faster runners.

A long lower leg provides space for large, powerful muscles used in running. *Ornithomimus* did have large, long leg muscles. From fossils, we can see the marks they left on its lower leg bones. The muscles of the ornithomimid's hip connected to the upper part of the leg. These points of attachment allowed the dinosaur to pull its leg up quickly while running, giving it extra speed.

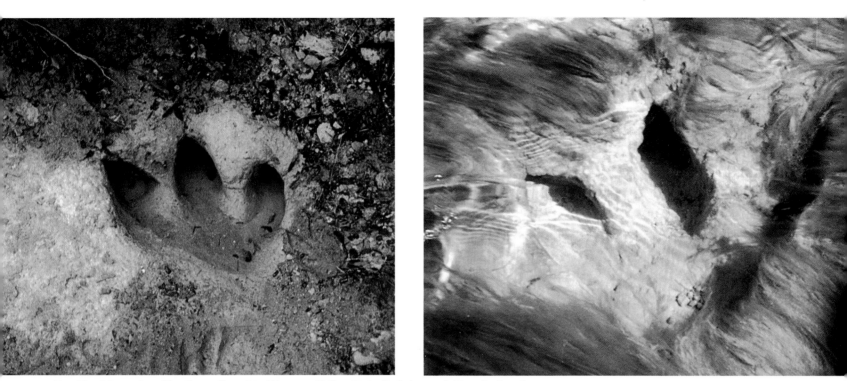

Fossilized footprints like these (found in Dinosaur Valley State Park in north Texas) give clues about the speed of dinosaurs.

Ornithomimids were definitely built for speed. But just how fast did *Ornithomimus* and its relatives run? Even though these animals are long dead, scientists have come up with some clever ways of estimating their running speed.

The best evidence for judging an ornithomimid's speed comes from fossil footprints. When an animal walks on soft ground, it leaves footprints behind. If mud or sand cover these footprints be-fore they are washed away and if they stay covered, the footprints can become fossils.

Scientists have found thousands of dinosaur footprints all over the world. It is difficult to know exactly which dinosaurs made which footprints. But some fossil footprints have been discovered that are shaped very much like the foot bones of ornithomimids.

One set of possible ornithomimid tracks in Texas have been closely studied by Dr. James Farlow. Dr. Farlow is a scientist who is very interested in how dinosaurs ran. He examined the fossil trackway in Texas and measured how far apart the footprints were from each other.

Dr. James Farlow (above left) and some of the dinosaur tracks he has studied

stride

left   right   left

The distance between two footprints on the same side of the body is an animal's **stride**—the length of each running step. The average stride for the dinosaur that made the Texas footprints was nearly 18 feet. The size of the footprints suggested that the animal was a medium-sized ornithomimid—about 12 feet long.

So each stride was longer than the dinosaur itself.

To make steps 18 feet apart, the animal had to be running very fast. Check it out yourself. When you walk, your steps are close together. The faster you run, the longer your stride becomes and the farther apart your footprints are.

right   left

Dr. McNeill Alexander

A Scottish scientist, McNeill Alexander, has developed a mathematical formula for figuring out a runner's speed from footprints. To use this formula, you need to know the length of the animal's leg as well as the length of its stride. Dr. Farlow used Dr. Alexander's formula to estimate the speed of the animal that made the Texas footprints. Assuming that the dinosaur had the leg length of a medium-sized ornithomimid, Dr. Farlow figures that it was running at a speed of at least 25 miles an hour.

Dr. Farlow has used emus like the one pictured above to test the formula that scientists use to make estimates of dinosaurs' speed.

To test the accuracy of the formula, Dr. Farlow has been trying it out on living animals. His test subjects are large birds, the animals most like ornithomimids. Dr. Farlow uses emus (EE-mooz) from a zoo. Like ostriches, these long-legged birds from Australia are runners rather than fliers.

To do the experiment, Dr. Farlow has to make an emu run across a stretch of muddy ground so that he can get some footprints. Emus are not very smart, and they don't like to follow Dr. Farlow's directions. He often has to chase a bird for a long time to make it run over the muddy ground. Sometimes both the emu and Dr. Farlow are exhausted before the experiment is over.

When Dr. Farlow finally gets a good set of footprints, he measures the length of the stride. He also measures the size of the emu. Then, using Dr. Alexander's formula, he makes an estimate of how fast the bird was running.

These tracks, found in Texas, were made by a fast-running dinosaur in the Cretaceous period. The dinosaur may have been an ornithomimid.

A model based on what scientists think *Struthiomimus* looked like

Dr. Farlow checks his estimate against a timed movie of the bird's run that measures its speed exactly. The movie works like the radar gun that police officers use to check a car's speed on the highway. So far, the speed estimates from Dr. Alexander's formula and the times from the movie match up pretty well. At least for the emu, the formula for judging speed from footprints works.

Based on Dr. Farlow's experiment, 25 miles per hour might be an accurate speed for one ornithomimid that ran across the mud in Texas many millions of years ago. But of course, we can't be sure that the dinosaur was an ornithomimid or that it was running at top speed.

We may never know just how fast *Ornithomimus* and its close cousins were. But if you are somehow transported back to dinosaur times, you had better hope that *Ornithomimus* isn't on the scene. If the dinosaur is there, hope that it doesn't look at you as lunch. Because even if you were as fast as the fastest human in the world, chances are you could never outrun an ornithomimid, the fastest dinosaur of all.

Glossary

carnivores: animals whose diet consists mainly of meat

Cretaceous period: a period of Earth's history that lasted from about 144 million years ago until about 65 million years ago

fossil: the remains of a formerly living thing or its parts, usually preserved in rock or soil

herbivorous: living on a diet of plants

omnivores: animals whose diet consists of a variety of foods including meat and plants

Pangaea: a name scientists use to describe the single land mass that once existed on Earth, before breaking apart to form the separate continents that now exist

predators: animals that hunt and kill other animals

stride: the length between steps made on the same side of an animal's body

theropod: a type of dinosaur that eats meat and typically has narrow feet with three large toes

Pronunciation Guide

Allosaurus (al-uh-SAW-rus)
Brachiosaurus (brayk-ee-oh-SAW-rus)
Compsognathus (komp-sug-NAY-thus)
Cretaceous (krih-TAY-shus)
Deinonychus (dy-no-NIH-kus)
Diplodocus (dih-PLOD-uh-kus)
Dromiceiomimus (dro-me-see-oh-MY-mus)
Edmontosaurus (ed-mon-tuh-SAW-rus)
emus (EE-mooz)
Gallimimus (gal-lih-MY-mus)
Harpymimus (har-pee-MY-mus)
Kentrosaurus (ken-truh-SAW-rus)
Maiasaura (my-uh-SAW-ruh)
ornithomimids (OR-nith-oh-MY-midz)
Ornithomimus velox (OR-nith-oh-MY-mus VEE-loks)
Orodromeus (oro-DRO-me-us)
Pangaea (pan-JEE-uh)
Stegoceras (ste-GOS-uh-rus)
Struthiomimus (stroo-theo-MY-mus)
Timimus (ti-MY-mus)
Triceratops (try-SER-uh-tops)
Tyrannosaurus rex (tuh-RAN-nuh-saw-rus REKS)

Index

Photo Acknowledgments:

Photographs are reproduced through the courtesy of: Royal Tyrrell Museum of Palaeontology/Alberta Community Development, pp. 8, 21 (top and bottom left), 38; Anne B. Keiser, p. 12; Department Library Services, American Museum of Natural History, pp. 13 (both), 16, 17; Photo of *Ornithomimus,* reproduced with permission of the Canadian Museum of Nature, p. 14; Wojciech Skarzynski, p. 20; Museum of Victoria, p. 21 (bottom right); Lynn M. Stone, p. 23; Thomas C. Boyden, p. 25; Royal Ontario Museum, Toronto, Canada, p. 27; Eugene Lajan/Dinosaur Valley State Park, p. 30 (both); Dr. James Farlow/Indiana University-Purdue University at Fort Wayne, pp. 31 (both), 35; Mr. A. Holliday, University of Leeds, p. 33; The Australian Overseas Information Service, p. 34.